Somewhere ANGELS

Be careful.
Don't think these little children are worth nothing.
I tell you that they have angels in heaven
who are always with my Father in heaven.

MATTHEW 18:10

For Dad & Mom...
Who Showed Me The Way

Somewhere ANGELS

By Larry Libby • Illustrations by Tim Jonke

Gold 'n' Honey
BOOKS

The author gratefully acknowledges his valued colleagues,
Carol Bartley and Thomas Womack,
for their insights, encouragement, and skillful editing of this book.

SOMEWHERE ANGELS
Published by Gold'n'Honey Books
a part of the Questar publishing family
© 1994 Questar Publishers, Inc.

International Standard Book Number: 0-88070-651-1

Printed in USA
Unless otherwise indicated, all Scripture references are from the International Children's Bible;
New Century Version © 1986, 1988 by Word Publishing; used by permission.

Scripture references marked NIV are from the Holy Bible: New International Version, c 1973, 1978, 1984 by the International
Bible Society. Used by permission of Zondervan Bible Publishers.

Scripture references marked SLB are from The Simplified Living Bible,
© 1990. Used by permission of Tyndale House Publishers, Inc.
All rights reserved.

Scripture references marked The Amplified Bible are from
The Amplified Bible © 1965 by Zondervan Publishing House.

For information: Questar Publishers, Box 1720, Sisters, Oregon 97759

LIBRARY OF CONGRESS CATALOGING-IN-PUBLICATION DATA
Libby, Larry
Somewhere angels / by Larry Libby.
p. cm.
ISBN 0-88070-651-1 :$13.99
1. Angels--Juvenile literature.   2. Guardian angels--Juvenile literature.
[1. Angels.] I. Title.   94-11230
BT966.2.L45 1994   CIP
235' .3--dc20   AC

98 99 00 01 02 — 10 9 8 7 6

Would Angels Like this Book?

One thing you can be pretty sure about…angels aren't too excited about angel books.
Angels, you see, don't like to be the center of attention.
Angels may not even like having people *think* about them very much.

Do you know why?

Because angels live for only one reason. With all their angel hearts, they long to please and serve God.
Angels live to obey God's commands and do EXACTLY what He says as fast and as well as they possibly can.
(And angels are *very* fast and *very* good at what they do.)

"What's the point of a book about *us?*" an angel might say. "We're only God's helpers, just like you. We do only what He says.
We go only where He sends. We say only what He tells us.
Write your book about your Heavenly Father and King Jesus—if you have to write another book at all.
Why get all excited about the King's messengers when you could talk about the King! There is SO MUCH to say
and sing about our good and strong and beautiful and wise and holy Lord!"
(Angels really can go *on and on* about these things.)

Well, I wouldn't want to have any angels upset with me, and I want to please the Lord, too!
So I'd like this book to be the kind even an angel wouldn't mind (too much). I would like to look at what God Himself says about
angels in the Bible. After all, if He's put this information about angels in His Book, He must want us to learn as much as we can.
And what we can best learn from angels is how to obey and worship God.

As we think about these bright, bold messengers from Heaven,
I'd like us to understand more and more about the God of all men and women and angels, who wants people on
Earth to love His Son and find His wonderful gift of forgiveness and eternal life.

That kind of book, I think, would make even the angels happy.

At least I hope so.

ANGELS CAN HELP
US WHEREVER WE ARE

❧

*Suddenly
an angel came to
him and
touched him.
"Get up and eat,"
the angel said.*

1 KINGS 19:5

No matter where you live, no matter how far you travel from home, no matter how alone you feel…you're always right next to Heaven's front door.

It doesn't matter if you are an astronaut out in space. It doesn't matter if you are a sailor deep under the ocean in a submarine.

God's angels can find you and help you wherever you are. Things like walls and oceans and mountains and locked doors don't even slow them down. When God sends an angel to find you or help you, the angel doesn't need a map or a road atlas or a phone book. He doesn't have to stop at a gas station and ask for directions. God always knows just where you are and just what you are doing. (Think about *that* the next time you're about to slug your little brother!)

Once an angel found the prophet Elijah sleeping under a tree in the desert. Elijah had been running hard and fast to escape the evil King Ahab and Queen Jezebel. When he finally crawled under the low branches of that scrawny tree and curled up to go to sleep, he thought he was all alone.

But he wasn't.

The Bible says: *Suddenly an angel came to him and touched him. "Get up and eat," the angel said. Elijah saw near his head a loaf baked over coals and a jar of water, so he ate and drank. Then he went back to sleep.*

Later the LORD'S angel came to him a second time. "Get up

and eat. If you don't, the journey will be too hard for you." So Elijah got up and ate and drank. The food made him strong enough to walk for forty days and nights to Mount Sinai, the mountain of God (1 Kings 19:5-8).*

Elijah found someone shaking him. Who was it? An enemy? King Ahab with a big spear? Queen Jezebel with her long, sharp fingernails? No, it was an angel from Heaven. He shook Elijah awake.

Elijah must have been surprised. It's not every day an angel comes around to wake you from your nap. And…*what was that delicious smell?*

Fresh-baked bread! In the middle of the desert!

The angel had baked a loaf of bread over the coals of a fire. And right alongside it was a jar of clear, cool water to drink. Elijah had been so tired he may have forgotten how hungry and thirsty he was…until he smelled that heavenly bread! You might have wished for a pepperoni pizza and a foamy mug of root beer. But Elijah was glad to get bread and water.

How do you think angel-baked bread would taste? Light and fluffy? Sweet and buttery? Would it melt in your mouth like a snowflake? Whatever it tasted like, this was no ordinary bread. After two meals of it, plus two naps and the sweet water from Heaven's well, Elijah got up and walked for *forty days*. Wouldn't angel bread be great stuff to have on a backpack trip? One piece of angel toast for breakfast and you wouldn't have to eat again for nearly a month and a half!

Elijah must have been glad God sent an angel to find him under that tree. But the truth is, God never lost him. God knows very well how to keep everything that belongs to Him.

WHY CAN'T WE SEE ANGELS?

✦

I always pray the God of our Lord Jesus Christ, the Father of Glory, that He may grant you a spirit of wisdom and revelation…by having the eyes of your heart flooded with light, so that you can know and understand the hope to which He has called you (Ephesians 1:17,19, Amplified Bible).

Why can't we see angels?

Maybe we *could* see angels…if we had the right kind of eyes. Oh, what we could see with the right kind of eyes!

We would see things that would surprise us.

We would see things that would fill us with courage.

That's what happened to a servant of the prophet Elisha. He got up one morning, stretched, yawned, and went outside to watch the sunrise. But what he saw made his sleepy eyes fly wide open with fear. All around the city, as far as he could see in the morning sunlight, enemy soldiers filled the streets and covered the hills.

He was nearly scared to death—just as you and I would have been. There wasn't just one or two or three enemy soldiers, but a whole *army*. No wonder that servant stumbled back into the house, trembling and crying to Elisha, "Oh, my master, what can we do?"

Elisha said, "Don't be afraid. The army that fights for us is larger than the one against us." Then Elisha prayed, "LORD, open my servant's eyes, and let him see."

The LORD opened the eyes of the young man, and he saw that the mountain was full of horses and chariots of fire all around Elisha" (2 Kings 6:16-17).

Elisha had the right kind of eyes.

Elisha wasn't afraid because he saw *more* than his servant saw. Behind and above that enemy army, he saw another, BIGGER army. It was an army of angel soldiers from Heaven, riding in chariots pulled by horses of fire. (Did you know there will be horses in Heaven?)

Elisha's servant couldn't see the angels. He couldn't see flaming horses and chariots in the sky. All he could see were things that made him afraid. All he could see were things that made his heart feel heavy and sad.

But God did something special for that young man. He gave him a new kind of eyes. He gave him what the Bible calls "eyes of the heart."

Have you ever felt the way Elisha's servant felt that morning? Sort of small…hardly big enough to count at all? Did you ever feel afraid of someone or something that seemed so much stronger than you? Did you ever feel as if you'd lost the race before anyone even said "Go"?

If only you had the right kind of eyes! If only you had "eyes of the heart"! Then you would see the Lord Jesus walking beside you. You would see His mighty angels ready to protect you and help you and fight enemies you don't even know about. You would see Heaven's armies riding across the hilltops and treetops and rooftops, swords and shields gleaming red and gold in the rising sun, bigger than all the armies of Earth put together.

The Lord opened the eyes of the young man…
2 KINGS 6:17

5

I know a little boy from the city who used to be afraid to stay overnight at his grandparents' house. They lived far out in the country with wide fields and deep forest all around their old white ranch house. The days were fun, of course, because there was a creek to fish and woods to explore and grand old apple trees to climb and even blue-tailed lizards to catch as they scurried among the rocks.

But nights were scary for this little boy. Do you know why?

It's because there were no city lights or porch lights or street lights for many miles around. And that made it VERY dark. When his grandparents turned out the lights in the house, it was darker than he thought it could ever be. It was so dark a billion stars glittered hard and bright in an inky black sky. And it was so dark in the cold back bedroom he could waggle his fingers right in front of his eyes and not see anything at all!

He would hide under the smooth, heavy quilts on his bed and never peek his head out until morning—just in case he *might* see something in the dark he didn't want to see! Do you think he would have felt better if he could have seen an angel soldier or two standing guard by his bed?

If only that little boy would have had the right kind of eyes! He wouldn't have been afraid at all. Angels, you know, don't care if it's light or dark. The blackest night doesn't keep them from seeing just fine. The brightest light doesn't make them blink or squint. In the book of Revelation, John tells about one powerful angel who *stood in the sun* and it didn't bother him a bit.

Of course it didn't!

If you could stand with eyes wide open in front of God's fiery, blazing throne—which must be the brightest place there ever could be—then standing in the middle of the sun would be no problem at all. It wouldn't look any brighter than your little sister's night light.

We don't have angel eyes, of course. Dark bedrooms look black as can be, and we should *never* look at the sun because it would burn our eyes badly.

But you and I can ask God for a new way of seeing.

You and I can ask God for the right kind of eyes.

What kind of eyes? Eyes that read the Bible and believe EVERY WORD. Eyes that see all the kind, good things God does for us every day. Eyes that look at a tiny flower or a rainbow or a purple-and-pink sunset or even a funny bug and see that God's hand created it. You have to have eyes of the heart to do those things. You have to have eyes that see more than the ordinary things everybody else sees.

If you had eyes like that, could you *really* see angels sitting on your bed or standing strong and stern by your front door or charging around in a fiery chariot over the top of your school? Well, I don't know. But you would *know* that they were there, because you believe God! And you would know that the Lord Jesus never, never leaves you.

Not even for a moment.

Not even in the dark.

WHAT DO ANGELS LOOK LIKE?

✦

Have you ever stood close to a huge, thundering water-fall? Could you feel the rumble of it in your chest? Did it give you a funny feeling in your stomach—to be so close to something so powerful and dangerous? Somehow it seemed beautiful and scary all at the same time, didn't it?

That's how angels look when they appear to people on Earth. They have a beauty that almost makes you afraid. Since Heaven is their home, the blazing brightness of that shining land clings to their clothing and their faces and even their words. No matter what you've read or what pictures you've seen, always remember that angels are *never* "cute" or "soft" or "funny" or "cuddly." They are servants of the Most High God—powerful and awesome, and sometimes stern.

One time a man named Daniel had been feeling troubled and worried. He was standing by a large river in the land of Babylon, just watching the water flow by, when he looked up and saw an angel.

Now you might think that would be just fine. You might think if it had been you, you would have said, "Hi there, Mr. Angel. Sit on this bank with me awhile and let's watch the fish jump." But Daniel was terribly afraid, even though he was always a brave man. Listen to what he said about it.

While standing there, I looked up and saw a man dressed in linen clothes with a belt of fine gold wrapped around his waist. His body was like shiny yellow quartz. His face was bright like light-ning, and his eyes were like fire. His arms and legs were shiny like polished bronze, and his voice sounded like the roar of a crowd.

I, Daniel, was the only person who saw the vision. The men with me did not see it, because they were so frightened that they ran away and hid. So I was left alone, watching this great vision. I lost my strength, my face turned white like a dead person, and I was helpless (Daniel 10:5-9).

Wow! I think I might have been right with those guys who ran and hid in the bushes! Or maybe I would have jumped in the river and swum like crazy.

For Daniel, there was no mistaking it—this angel looked like an angel.

There are other times in the Bible, however, when angels look just like people. Here's what Abraham saw one day when he was sitting by the door of his tent.

He looked up and saw three men standing near him. When Abraham saw them, he ran from his tent to meet them. He bowed facedown on the ground before them and said, "Sir, if you think well of me, please stay awhile with me, your servant. I will bring some water so all of you can wash your feet. You may rest under the tree, and I will get some bread for you so you can regain your strength. Then you may continue on your journey."

The three men said, "That is fine. Do as you said" (Genesis 18:2-5).

But these three men weren't men at all, as you will discover if you read the rest of that story from the Bible (and I hope you do!). Abraham's three visitors were really God and two angels in the form of human beings.

Did Abraham know these were guests from Heaven when he treated them with respect and kindness and invited them for

When Jacob also went his way, the angels of God met him.

GENESIS 32:1

7

lunch? Perhaps at first he didn't, but in time he did. (By the way, I'll bet those angels politely ate everything on their plates at Abraham's house.)

The book of Hebrews tells us something amazing:

Keep on loving each other as brothers and sisters. Remember to welcome strangers, because some who have done this have welcomed angels without knowing it (Hebrews 13:1-2).

Would you like to have an angel over to your house for dinner?

Would you like to have a picnic in the park with an angel?

Would you like to serve angel-food cake and strawberries to an angel?

Would you like to watch a California Angels baseball game and share your popcorn and orange soda with a *real* angel?

The Bible says people have actually done things like this—without even knowing it! The writer of Hebrews says to keep on loving the people who love Jesus. But don't stop there! When you have a chance, help people you don't even know. Have people over to your house who need a meal or some friendly company. Invite new neighbors to some of your family hikes and barbecues and game nights and fun times. Welcome people into your home the way Jesus always welcomed people.

And guess what?

One of those times you might find yourself being friendly to people who aren't people at all, but visitors from Heaven.

You may never know it until you finally get to Heaven. Just imagine yourself sitting along some clear, bubbling stream that comes chattering and singing out of the green heavenly hills.

Then an angel walks up and sits beside you and calls you by name. (In Heaven, of course, that wouldn't scare you at all. But it might make you sit up a little straighter.)

"Hello, sir," you would say. "I'm happy to meet you."

"Oh," the angel might laugh, "we've met before."

"Really? Then I'm happy for that, too. But I can't remember when."

"Don't you remember the Monopoly game and the banana splits we had in your living room that November night—back on Old Earth? You were so kind to me. You welcomed me in the name of King Jesus. Then you spilled your hot chocolate on my foot! But I had two hotels on Boardwalk and took all your money."

"Monopoly? Boardwalk? Bananas? What do you—OH! *Now* I remember! Do you mean—*you're* Mr. Matumbo, the African exchange student?"

"Yes, I believe that's what you called me when you welcomed me into your home. And now, my young friend, I get to welcome you to *my* home!"

Remember to welcome strangers, because some who have done this have welcomed angels without knowing it.
HEBREWS 13:2

9

WILL I BE AN ANGEL WHEN I DIE?

Will we be angels when we die? You or I couldn't be angels even if we wanted to be! We couldn't be angels even if we were the kindest, best-hearted people who ever lived.

Now I know that daddies sometimes call mommies "angel" and grownups sometimes say children have been "little angels" (if those children have been extra good), but people can never *really* be angels. Not here. Not in Heaven. Not anywhere.

Do you know why? Because angels are angels and people are people. We're different—but each special in our own way.

Angels are like older brothers who came along first. God created His strong, starbright angels before there was ever an Earth or people to live on it. Later—and God doesn't tell us how much later—He scooped up some soil in the Garden of Eden and carefully shaped the first human being.

The Bible says that everyone who belongs to the Lord Jesus gets to live with God and the angels in Heaven—for always and forever. But even in Heaven we'll be different from the angels.

As far as we know, angels have always lived in Heaven—they've never known another home. *But we human beings will leave an old home and move into a shimmering, sparkling new Home more beautiful than we could ever dream or imagine.*

Angels have always had the same made-for-Heaven bodies. *But we will leave our old bodies behind and step into strong, new, made-for-Heaven bodies—very different from what we have now.*

Angels are called "winds," "servants," "flames of fire," and "morning stars." *But we will be called sons and daughters of God.*

Angels have always belonged to King Jesus. *But we cannot belong to Jesus until He becomes our own Savior and Lord—and then we belong to Him forever.*

Angels look at the nail scars in the hands and feet of Jesus with wonder and amazement. *But we will look at those scars and say, "I know what those are and I know why they are there. He died for me—so that I could be here with Him."*

I don't know about you, but I wonder if we will have angel friends and angel neighbors in Heaven…

Will I be able to play marbles or checkers or shoot baskets with an angel—and who would win?

Will I have angels over for dinner—and what would they especially like to eat?

Will angels show me their favorite places on Heaven's bright hilltops or along Heaven's crystal rivers—or will they be too busy running errands for God?

Will angels live near my own special place in Heaven—where I can wave at them out my window—or will they live in their own angel cities? (And will they ever invite me over to *their* house?)

I'm saving up a lot of questions for Heaven, aren't you? I'm glad God has answers for every question that could ever be.

HOW DO ANGELS
GET TO EARTH FROM HEAVEN?

Jacob left Beersheba and set out for Haran. When he came to a place, he spent the night there because the sun had set. He found a stone and laid his head on it to go to sleep. Jacob dreamed that there was a ladder resting on the earth and reaching up into heaven, and he saw angels of God going up and coming down the ladder. Then Jacob saw the LORD standing above the ladder, and he said, "I am the LORD, the God of Abraham your grandfather, and the God of Isaac" (Genesis 28: 10-13).

Is there really a ladder that reaches up to Heaven?

Is there…

    a stairway?

        An elevator?

        An escalator?

(I know a little girl who once got the toe of one of her brand new pink tennis shoes caught in an escalator. She lost almost half of her shoe but got to keep all of her toes!)

What do you think Jacob's dream about that ladder means? I think the Bible is saying that Heaven and Earth are *linked*. Heaven is Up and Earth is Down, but you can get from There to Here and from Here to There. God cares very much about what happens on our world. So angels care, too. They live in Heaven, but they visit the Earth whenever He sends them.

Jacob's dream about the ladder may have been God's way of saying, "Jacob, you may feel all by yourself and afraid. You may feel everyone is against you. But you are not alone. You don't have to face your enemies alone. The door to Heaven is open, not closed. My angels are always going back and forth from Heaven, obeying my commands. I will help you and be with you, Jacob, because I love you. My angels will help you and guard you because I tell them to."

The next morning, when Jacob woke up, he was amazed as he remembered his dream. He named the place where he had slept that night "The House of God," because it seemed that he had somehow found Heaven's front door.

But the truth is…Heaven's front door is wherever God *wants* it to be.

Heaven's front door could be your own bedside where you kneel to pray.

Heaven's front door could be in your church, where you study the Bible and sing praise to God.

Heaven's front door could be at the playground, where you sit on top of the jungle gym and watch the shapes of clouds and think about your heavenly Father.

Heaven's front door is anywhere God wants to open it. And sometimes, He sends His angels through that door. They always want to come—fast as lightning—because they just *love* running errands for God.

Jacob dreamed there was a ladder… reaching up into heaven.

GENESIS 28:12

13

WHEN IS AN ANGEL
MORE THAN AN ANGEL?

A man named Manoah lived with his wife in a town called Zorah, in Israel. One day the Angel of the Lord appeared to Manoah's wife and told her she was going to have a baby.

Well, as you might imagine, she was very excited. She ran as fast as she could run to tell her husband everything that had happened.

She said, "A man from God came to me. He looked like an angel from God; his appearance was frightening. I didn't ask him where he was from, and he didn't tell me his name" *(Judges 13:6).*

Manoah wanted to see this Angel, too. He prayed to the Lord and asked for the Angel to come back. And He did! Manoah's wife had been sitting out in the field, (waiting for an angel, I'll bet) and suddenly, there He was! (I think the middle of a golden field might be a nice place to meet an angel, don't you?)

Manoah's wife was thrilled. Her heart pounded so hard. She probably told the Angel, "Please, sir—wait just a minute! Please don't move! Please don't fly away! I'll be *right back*!" Then she picked up her skirts and ran as fast as she could back to the house for her husband. (Why did Manoah always have to be inside reading the paper while Mrs. Manoah was meeting angels out in the field? Maybe he should have been waiting in the field with her!)

Mrs. Manoah must have burst through the door all red-faced and out of breath.

"He is here! The man who appeared to me the other day is here!"

Manoah got up and followed his wife. When he came to the man he said, "Are you the man who spoke to my wife?"

The man said, "I am" *(Judges 13:10-11).*

They talked to the Angel for a while and then asked Him to stay for supper. The Bible says Manoah still didn't know or understand who this visitor was! (I wonder if his wife had the right kind of eyes, and he didn't.)

The angel of the LORD answered, "Even if I stay awhile, I would not eat your food. But if you want to prepare something, offer a burnt offering to the LORD."

Then Manoah asked the angel of the LORD, "What is your name? Then we will honor you when what you have said really happens."

The angel of the LORD said, "Why do you ask my name? It is too amazing for you to understand." So Manoah sacrificed a young goat on a rock and offered some grain as a gift to the LORD. Then an amazing thing happened as Manoah and his wife watched. The flames went up to the sky from the altar. As the fire burned, the angel of the LORD went up to heaven in the flame. When Manoah and his wife saw that, they bowed facedown on the ground...Then Manoah understood that the man was really the angel of the LORD. Manoah said, "We have seen God, so we will surely die" *(Judges 13:16-22).*

But of course they didn't die. God blessed them with a baby boy who grew up to be the strongest man who ever was. (But that's another story!)

"A man from God came to me. He looked like an angel from God."

JUDGES 13:6

15

Manoah and Mrs. Manoah knew their visitor was more than a man.

They knew He was more than an angel.

Manoah said, "We have seen *God*!" And he was right. Their visitor—this "Angel of the Lord"—was God Himself.

These things are very mysterious! But men and women who have studied the Bible for many years say that in Old Testament times, God used to visit people from time to time in the form of a shining angel. Some of these wise people say this "Angel of the Lord" was Jesus Himself, visiting the world He would one day come to live in for a little while as a human being.

Just think…when He came to Zorah and called on Mrs. Manoah, He was only thirteen miles from Bethlehem, where He would be born in a little stable on a starlit night. (I wonder if He thought about that!)

But after Jesus became a man and lived here with us on our world, we don't hear any more about this "Angel of the Lord." Maybe that's because Jesus Himself is with us always! He has said, "I will never leave you; I will never forget you" and "I will be with you always, until the end of this age" (Matthew 28:20; Hebrews 13:5;).

When the Lord Jesus came to Earth on that first Christmas so long ago, He didn't come as a mighty angel. He came as a tiny, red-faced baby boy.

After that happened, nothing in Earth or Heaven could ever be the same.

ANGELS DELIVER!

Have you ever watched a mail carrier or a delivery person carrying a whole armload of parcels and packages? These men and women work hard in all kinds of weather to get those brown-wrapped boxes and bulky envelopes to the right house and the right people at the right time.

That's important, of course, to the person who might be waiting for a package. But it could be even more important to the person who *sent* it!

Think of a grandmother who pours so much Grandmother Love into a carefully wrapped box of home-made, white-frosted, snowman cookies. She can't wait for all that love to get to a certain grandson in a faraway city. As soon as the package is opened and the first sweet cookie gets grabbed by a little hand, that Grandmother Love bubbles up out of the box and splashes across the room like morning sunshine.

Think of a young wife who proudly tucks pictures of her new baby into a package. Somewhere in the middle of a distant ocean, in the tiny cabin of a big Navy ship, a lonesome sailor daddy is waiting and waiting for a picture of a little daughter he has never seen. And when he opens that package, the love and happiness he feels makes him want to run up and down every ladder in that ship yelling, "Look at this! Look at this! Oh, she's *beautiful*!"

Ever since God made men and women to live on this world, He has used His strong, swift angels as letter carriers and delivery persons. I guess if angels drove big white trucks between

Heaven and Earth, the gold letters on the side of those shiny trucks might read H.P.S. (Heaven's Parcel Service).

In the Bible, Jacob received a package from H.P.S. just when he needed it most.

When Jacob also went his way, the angels of God met him. When he saw them, he said, "This is the camp of God!" So he named that place…two camps (Genesis 32:1).

Do you know what sort of package those angels brought to Jacob from God? It wasn't a box of cookies—as good as heavenly cookies might be. It was a big bundle of encouragement.

Jacob had been scared and worried. He might have even begun to wonder if God still loved him. So God sent His delivery angels with their arms full of hope, fresh from Heaven (where everyone has plenty of hope to spare). Jacob looked around at his own camp, then realized that God's angels were camped right alongside! Of course Jacob felt encouraged. How could anyone be sad or worried with a troop of angels so close you could see them around their campfires! (I wonder what the angels did in *their* camp? Do you suppose they sang songs or roasted marshmallows?)

One dark night many years after Jacob, the H.P.S. had a very special job. The disciple Peter was in King Herod's jail. That evil king wanted to kill Peter for telling so many people about the real King, Jesus Christ. So Peter's friends had been praying for him through the long night. They didn't know God would surprise them by delivering Peter right to their door!

In the middle of the night, when everyone was asleep, God sent a delivery angel to deliver Peter out of jail! The only trouble was, the angel couldn't get Peter to wake up!

Peter was sleeping between two soldiers, bound with two chains. Other soldiers were guarding the door of the jail. Suddenly, an angel of the Lord stood there, and a light shined in the cell. The angel struck Peter on the side and woke him up. "Hurry! Get up!" the angel said. And the chains fell off Peter's hands. Then the angel told him, "Get dressed and put on your sandals." And Peter did. Then the angel said, "Put on your coat and follow me."

So Peter followed him out, but he did not know if what the angel was doing was real; he thought he might be seeing a vision. They went past the first and second guards and came to the iron gate that separated them from the city. The gate opened by itself for them, and they went through it. When they had walked down one street, the angel suddenly left him (Acts 12:6-10).

The angel had to smack Peter on the ribs to wake him up. He'd been sleeping and snoring away between those two soldiers just as if he were tucked in his own bed.

"Hurry!" the angel told Peter. "Get up!"

Peter mumbled and blinked and yawned. He was so sleepy the angel had to help him along. "Get dressed and put on your sandals." Sleepy Peter tied on his sandals, his hands fumbling at the thongs. "Put on your coat and follow me." Now where was that coat? Do you suppose the angel had to hold the coat while Peter slipped it on? *"Hurry, Peter, hurry! Wake up, Peter! Get your shoes on, Peter. Get your coat on, Peter. Follow me, Peter."*

Don't you wish an angel could help you get ready for school and deliver you to the bus stop in the morning? You would NEVER miss the bus!

"So men, have courage. I trust in God that everything will happen as his angel told me."
ACTS 27:25

17

Angels deliver whatever God wants to send. Lots of times, what He wants to send is a big package of hope and love.

That's the sort of package God sent one night to the missionary Paul. Paul was a prisoner of Roman soldiers, who were taking him across the sea to Rome on a sailing ship. A big, scary storm had been shaking and shoving that ship for days and days. The sky boiled with dark clouds. The wild wind howled endlessly—until they all thought they'd go crazy. Men on the ship began to wonder if everyone was going to die. They were almost ready to give up.

That's when Paul had a visit from a delivery angel. Just listen to what he told everyone the next morning:

"Last night an angel came to me from the God I belong to and worship. The angel said, 'Paul, do not be afraid. You must stand before Caesar. And God has promised you that he will save the lives of everyone sailing with you.' So men, have courage. I trust in God that everything will happen as his angel told me" (Acts 27:23-26).

That H.P.S. delivery angel had no trouble finding Paul in the damp darkness under the deck of that little ship. Even in the middle of the sea! Even in the middle of the night! Even in the middle of a wild storm! When God wants to send hope and help to His people, angels just roll up their sleeves and get it done.

Have you ever received a big box of hope, fresh from Heaven? I'll bet you have. And just because you didn't *see* the delivery angel doesn't mean he wasn't there.

Angels, you know, have lots to do and lots of deliveries to make. And they don't wait around for tips or handshakes or thank-you's.

Doing God's will is all the reward they want or need.

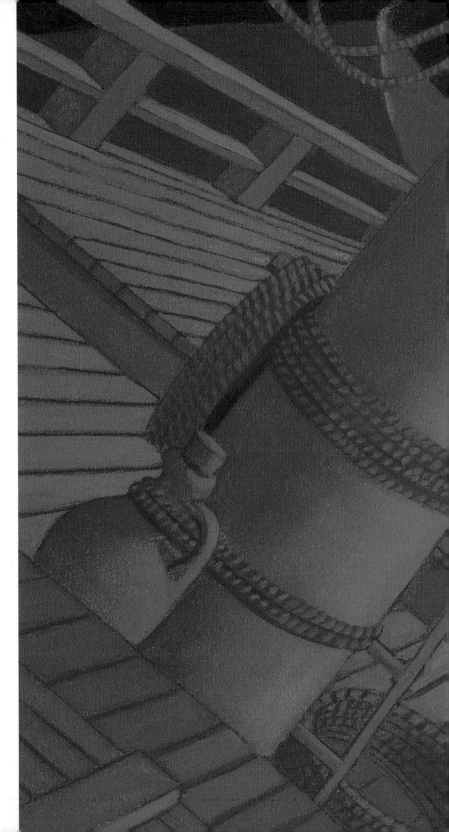

ARE ANGELS HAPPIER THAN PEOPLE?

❧

Direct me
in the path of your
commands,
for there I find
delight.

PSALM 119:35, NIV

20

Along time ago, a good man sat down and wrote out this little prayer to God: *Direct me in the path of your commands, for there I find delight (Psalm 119:35, NIV).*

That man was never happier than when he was obeying God. Life was never sweeter and the days never brighter than when he was doing just what God wanted him to do.

He called it "finding delight."

What is "delight"?

Delight is a frosty ice cream bar on a hot summer afternoon. Delight is a snapping, popping, red-and-orange fire in the fireplace and a mug of hot chocolate on a cold, rainy night. Delight is opening a present and finding something you've wanted (but hardly dared hope for) for a long, long time. Delight is seeing your best friend smiling at your front door after she's been on vacation for a *whole week.*

When this man obeyed God, just getting up in the morning was "delight." Food tasted tastier, the wind smelled fresher, the grass looked greener, the sun felt warmer, the bed felt softer, the air felt lighter, and songs seemed somehow easier to whistle. That's why he was praying, "Dear Lord, help me to *always* walk the way You want me to walk. Help me to *always* have this happy feeling I feel when my life pleases You."

Now the problem is, you and I don't always do what God wants us to do, and we lose that happy feeling of delight. But what about angels? Angels ALWAYS obey God. Angels ALWAYS do just what He wants. Does that mean they're happy and joyful? Does that mean they really like being angels?

Yes, it does.

It's exciting to be one of God's special helpers. You could talk to every angel in Heaven and never find one who was bored or had a bad day or wanted to stay in bed or wished it was Friday.

But here's something amazing. You and I can be happy in a way no angel in Heaven ever can! It's true. Only human beings can know and feel the great happiness and thankfulness of being *rescued* by God.

Angels have never been rescued.

Angels have never had to be saved by God.

Angels have never felt God's strong hand pulling them out of terrible trouble.

Only girls and boys and men and women can feel the relief and joy and *delight* of having their sins forgiven! Washed away forever! We could have NEVER loved Jesus if He hadn't reached out to help us. We could NEVER go to Heaven if Jesus hadn't come all the way *from* Heaven to rescue us.

Because of those things, angels can't look at the Lord Jesus in quite the same way we can. When angels look at Jesus they see a powerful, awesome Master, shooting out bright beams of glory into the farthest corners of the Universe. They see the greatest and mightiest King of all Kings. AND HE IS! Oh yes, He is! We'd best remember that.

But you and I can look at Jesus and also see...

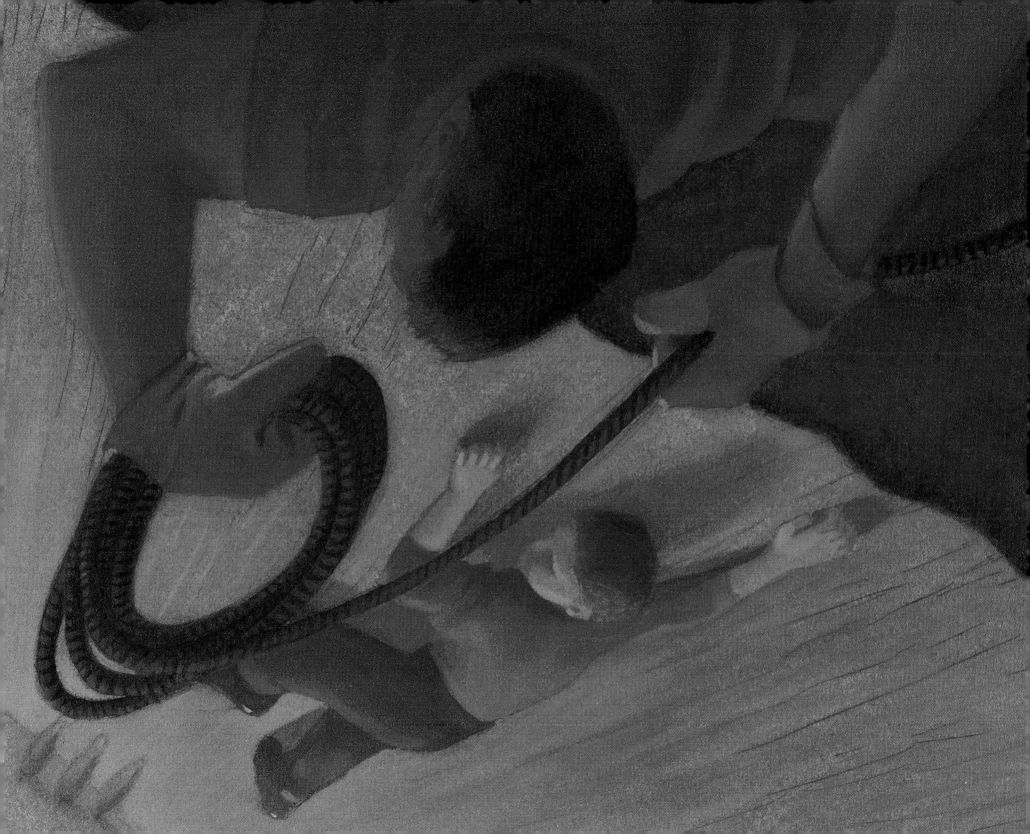

a Best Friend
a Big Brother
a Kind and Patient Helper
and—most of all—
a Rescuer
…a Savior.

I don't know about you, but that makes me awfully happy. As happy as an angel? Well, I can't answer that. But I'm plenty happy enough for *me*.

DO YOU AND I HAVE A SPECIAL ANGEL OF OUR OWN?

Do you and I have a special angel of our own? Many people who have studied the Bible for years believe that we do. They believe it because of what Jesus once said to His twelve followers:

"Be careful. Don't think these little children are worth nothing. I tell you that they have angels in heaven who are always with my Father in heaven" (Matthew 18:10).

If each of us *does* have a special protector angel—a "guardian angel" to keep up with us—then I know some little boys and girls whose angels must really sweat! (I'm not sure at all that angels sweat, but—well, you know what I mean.) One boy I know had two broken arms, a broken thumb, a broken nose, and a broken big toe before he finally grew up. He broke so many pairs of glasses that his mom and dad lost count. Think

how hard his angel had to work to keep him from breaking something *really* important. It's a good thing angels don't get tired or need vacations or take time-outs!

When Jesus spoke those words about children's angels in Heaven, was He saying that every little boy has a strong angel watching over him? Was He saying that every little girl has a powerful protector angel keeping guard over her? That might have been what He meant.

But I know one thing He meant for sure.

Jesus cares very much about each and every boy and girl. He knows when a little child is hurt or treated badly by a grownup. He watches from Heaven and takes very careful notice—and so do His powerful angels. People who hurt children ought to be afraid of the Lord, because He will punish them.

Does He send His angels to watch over you and protect you and stay close to you? Yes, I think He does.

Does that mean you will never be hurt? Does that mean an angel will keep a little boy from falling off his bicycle or scraping his knee or cutting his finger or breaking his heart? Does that mean a little girl will never die and leave for Heaven before she has a chance to grow up? Does that mean an angel will keep other children from calling you names that *really* hurt your feelings?

No. There will still be hurts. Until we finally get home to Heaven, there will always be hurts.

But God will always help us and stay very near to us. God will never stop feeling our hurts and helping us be strong.

God loves to do those things. And sometimes, angels get to help.

The Lord saves those who fear him. His angel camps around them.

PSALM 34:7

23

ANGELS ARE STRONG FRIENDS

I am sending an angel ahead of you, who will protect you as you travel. He will lead you to the place I have prepared. Pay attention to the angel and obey him...my power is in him. If you carefully listen to all he says and do everything that I tell you, I will be an enemy to your enemies. I will fight all who fight against you. My angel will go ahead of you and take you into the land (Exodus 23:20-23).

I know a pastor from California who was visiting Washington, D.C. Early one morning he and his teenage daughter got dressed to go jogging. As they were riding in the hotel elevator, two strong-looking men got on. They were dressed to go jogging, too. After the pastor told them what he and his daughter were going to do, one of the men said, "Why don't you let us jog along with you? We'll make sure you're safe."

So the two men ran alongside the pastor and his girl. And the men's eyes were always looking this way and that, and no one bothered that little group of runners at all. Later, this pastor found out that their two new friends were the President's own Secret Service guards!

Angels are Heaven's Secret Service guards. And they are very good company to have.

A college student I know very well was driving down the freeway late at night in his little car when he fell asleep at the wheel. He woke up suddenly—just as the car was racing off the edge of the road. Before he could even think what to, the steering wheel jerked back the other way onto the road. He was safe—and very awake, by this time!

24

How did it happen? Did he do it himself? Did an angel grab the wheel? God could have helped him either way.

In the Bible, Daniel had some enemies who tricked the King of Persia into throwing Daniel into a dark pit full of hungry lions. Early the next morning, the sad and worried king came to the edge of the pit and called out to Daniel. Had this good man's God been able to save him? Imagine the king's surprise when he heard Daniel's strong, calm voice from the bottom of that pit.

"O king, live forever! My God has sent his angel to close the lions' mouths. They have not hurt me" (Daniel 6:22).

What caused those lions to change their minds about dining on Daniel? Did they lose their appetites? I don't think so! They were very hungry. The Bible says an angel "closed the lions' mouths."

Do you suppose the lions were surprised to find they couldn't open their mouths— just when they really wanted to? Do you think maybe the lions saw the angel and decided it might be best to leave Daniel alone? I think Daniel saw something, too, don't you? After all, he told King Darius, "God sent His angel."

Of course God doesn't always close the mouth of an animal that would like to bite us. I wish an angel would have helped *me* once when a big white dog ran up behind me and bit me right where I sit down. But one thing is for sure: the angel saved Daniel's life. And I think angels still save the lives of God's people, all over the world.

DID JESUS HAVE GUARDIAN ANGELS?

Angels watched over Jesus carefully while He was a man living on Earth. He was still their King! He was still their Lord! Even though He was living in the body of a man (which must have seemed strange to the angels), they all knew He was the mighty Son of God.

After Satan argued with Jesus and tried to trick Him into disobeying the Heavenly Father, Jesus must have been very, very tired. He had walked many hard miles through a rocky desert and hadn't had a single bite to eat for forty days. But as soon as Jesus won that fight with Satan, the angels were right there to care for Him.

How many angels?

Every one of them probably wanted to come.

If God had let it happen, Heaven might have emptied out in half a second. That desert wouldn't have been able to hold all the angels who wanted to come and help the Lord Jesus. There wouldn't have been enough room for a lizard to turn around.

So God the Father probably sent only a few angels.

But how did they care for Jesus? What did they do?

Did they give Him a cool drink? Did they fix Him a snack? Did they bring something good from Home for Him to eat? Did they make Him a soft bed with clean, cool sheets? Did they shade Him from the hot sun or cover Him in the cold desert night? Those angels would have done *anything* for their King.

A few years later, the Lord Jesus was in the most terrible time of His life. In a few hours He would have to die on the cross.

He knew that men who hated him were already on their way to take Him prisoner.

He knew that one of His close friends had turned against Him.

He knew that His helpers would all run away and leave Him alone.

He knew that He would soon have to die in the most dreadful way for the sins of everybody who would ever live.

Jesus must have felt sad and frightened and hurt and horribly lonely all at the same time. I don't think you and I could ever understand what Jesus felt in those dark moments. The Bible says:

He kneeled down and prayed, "Father, if you are willing, take away this cup of suffering. But do what you want, not what I want." Then an angel from heaven appeared to him to strengthen him. Being full of pain, Jesus prayed even harder. His sweat was like drops of blood falling to the ground (Luke 22:42).

There were no friends to help Jesus. Peter and John and the rest of them were sound asleep.

But an angel walked right through Heaven's front door and came alongside the Lord Jesus as He knelt in the dust.

What do you think that angel did?

Had any angel ever been bold enough to actually touch the robe of the King of Heaven? But now...the King's heart was broken! Now the King was in the weak body of a man. He needed someone to help, someone to care. Maybe that angel

So the devil left Jesus, and angels came and took care of him.
MATTHEW 4:11

27

very quietly and respectfully knelt down beside Jesus, his white angel robe trailing in the dust.

Maybe he whispered a message of love from the Father.

Maybe he actually dared to reach out a hand and rest it on the trembling shoulders of his great King.

Oh, how sad and sorrowful that messenger from Heaven must have been! I'm sure that angel would have (if he could have) gladly taken all of the Lord's pain and hurt and sorrow. I'm sure that angel would have (if he could have) said, "Don't cry, King Jesus. I will go to the cross for You. I'll let them hurt me and kill me. I'll let them beat up on me and spit on me and laugh at me. You go on back Home to Heaven where every-body misses you so much. Let me die here instead of You."

But no angel would have ever done that, no matter what his heart wanted to do. Angels can only obey the Father's wishes, and it was the Father's own plan that His dearly loved Son would die for you and me.

Only Jesus could save us.
Not an angel.
Not a hundred angels.
Not a million angels.
Not all the angels in Heaven.

So what could that one angel on that dark, dusty hillside do for a heart-broken Lord Jesus that night? What *could* he do but scoot up near his God and say, "We all love You and can't wait for You to come Home."

WHY DIDN'T ANGELS RESCUE JESUS FROM THE CROSS?

When men were coming to arrest Jesus, the Lord's friend Peter wanted to fight them. He pulled out a big sword and started swinging it around.

Of course, when you do something like that, someone is bound to get hurt. And someone did. A man named Malchus, the High Priest's helper, suddenly was missing an ear! But Jesus touched Malchus, and his ear was instantly back where it belonged.

Then Jesus said to Peter,

"Put your sword back in its place. All who use swords will be killed with swords. Surely you know I could ask my Father, and he would give me more than twelve armies of angels. But it must happen this way to bring about what the Scriptures say" (Matthew 26:52-54).

All Jesus had to do was say one word—*one litte word*—and He could have had a million powerful angels flash down from the night sky like a storm of falling stars.

Even *one* of those angels could have destroyed the whole Roman army.

Even *one* of those angels could have reached out his hand and melted the city of Jerusalem into a puddle.

What could an *army* of angels have done?

What could TWELVE ARMIES of angels have done?

I think those angels would have gladly destroyed the whole world to protect King Jesus, don't you?

But Jesus didn't want to fight. He didn't want to defend Himself. He knew He had come to Earth to die on a cross. He knew He had come to save the world, not destroy it. He knew that if the angels rescued Him (and oh! how they must have wanted to!), then you and I would never be able to know God or live with Him in Heaven. Because He loved you and me so much—that's why He wouldn't let the angels rescue Him. If *He* had been rescued, *we* could never, never have been rescued!

So He didn't call twelve armies of angels.

He didn't call one army of angels.

He didn't call even a single angel.

He wouldn't even let His friend—a scared, wild-eyed fisherman with a borrowed sword—cut off an enemy's ear!

Jesus took all the pain with no one to help. Jesus let Himself be lied about, beaten up, made fun of, and finally, nailed on a cross to die.

Can you imagine the angels hovering all around—wishing and wishing Jesus would let them fight the people who were hurting Him?

But Jesus wouldn't let them. He wouldn't let them lift a finger...or a wing. He wouldn't let them swing a sword (and their aim would have been much better than Peter's!). All He could think about were the boys and girls and men and women whom He could save by dying for them.

I think the angels learned something that night, don't you? I think the angels learned how much He loves us.

*Praise the Lord,
O heavens!
Praise him from
the skies!*

PSALMS 148:1

30

CAN WE PRAISE GOD WITH THE ANGELS?

*B*less the LORD, *you mighty angels. Bless him, you who carry out his orders. Praise him as you listen for each of his commands. Yes, bless the Lord, you armies of angels. Praise him, you who serve him all the time.*

Praise the LORD, O heavens! Praise him from the skies! Praise him, all his angels, all the armies of heaven (Psalms 103:20-21; 148:1-2, SLB).

Who wrote those words?

This psalm writer, who was just a man, called on the *angels* to praise their God! I'm sure the angels didn't mind a bit. They'll praise the Lord for any reason at all, and love doing it.

Do angels join with us when we thank and praise God with all our hearts? Do they sing too, in voices our ears can't hear?

I once heard a Christian singer talk about a worship meeting in cold, snowy Alaska. It was a night he would remember the rest of his life.

Outside, the winter wind moaned and hissed against the frosted church windows. But *inside* the little church, people were warm and happy and singing song after song of praise to God. No one wanted to stop. No one could remember a better worship time.

But something mysterious and wonderful happened that icy, starlit night. After one last praise song, they all finally stopped to catch their breath. The people stopped singing. The

musicians put down their instruments. But somehow, *the singing kept going*! Everyone heard it. The beautiful praise music kept rolling on and on for a little while, like a long, silvery echo. Was it an echo coming back from the high mountains of Heaven? Was it the voices of angels, who got so carried away in all that praise to God that they couldn't help singing along—and then didn't notice when everyone else stopped?

Why don't you try it sometime?

Sing the best praise song to the Lord Jesus that you know, and sing it with all your heart. Then, before you sing it again, call on a few angels to join you. (Maybe eight or ten or however many you think would sound good.) Say just what the man in the book of Psalms said: "Bless the Lord, you mighty angels! Praise the Lord, you armies of heaven!"

No matter what they're busy with, most of the angels I know about would love to jump in and join the song for a verse or two. (When you think about it, there is no more important work being done anywhere than praising God.)

Who knows, your little praise chorus might get something BIG started as more and more angels get caught up in the song. Then, by the time you've closed your eyes for the night, all of Heaven might be singing and ringing with the simple chorus that you started down in your own room. When the angels finally settle down and look around to see who started it all, there you would be, already snuggled down asleep in your bed.

Wouldn't that be a nice thought to fall asleep with?

The morning stars sang together and all the angels shouted with joy.
JOB 38:7

WHAT CAN WE LEARN FROM ANGELS?

Scientists all over the world spend zillions of dollars every year to search the dark corners of outer space. They send up rockets and satellites. They send out space shuttles and deep space probes and robot explorers. They build telescopes bigger than barns and stare at the stars until their eyes turn red. They aim huge listening machines at the sky—like the ears of a giant—and strain to hear every beep, whir, glurp, and twitter from faraway stars and planets.

Why do they do all these things?

Why do they work so hard and spend so much…looking and looking?

What are they looking for?

What are they listening for?

What do they want to find?

Some of them keep hoping and hoping that *someday* they will see or hear something from someone on another planet out in space. They would love to discover that the people on our little blue world are not ALL ALONE in this big cold universe.

Now you don't have to tell them I said so (and I wouldn't want to hurt their feelings, they *do* work so hard), but I think if they would just read their Bibles they might discover some amazing things.

They want to learn about aliens…but what about *angels*?

Angels, after all, are not from this world.

Angels are not human beings.

Angels are strong.

Angels are smart.

Angels are beautiful and good.

Angels can laugh and sing and light up the night.

Angels can fly and walk through walls and even step into people's dreams.

Angels are older than the Earth.

Angels watched the creation of our whole Universe. (And know just how it was done.)

Angels visit our planet all the time.

Angels can speak our language.

Angels have seen God's face, and know so much about Him.

In the Bible, scientists (and all of us) can learn so much about these wonderful "aliens." We can learn what angels have done long ago, what they are doing right now, and even what they *will* do in the future.

God has told us a great deal *about* angels. And even if it isn't as much as we would like to know, I think we could spend the rest of our lives trying to puzzle it through.

But even more important is what we can learn *from* angels. I can think of at least two things. (You can probably think of more.)

1. WE CAN LEARN THE GREAT JOY OF OBEYING GOD QUICKLY.

When God speaks, angels don't take time to think about it, ask questions, look at their watch, get a drink of water, or even tie their shoes. They just turn right around and DO IT. God says it and—*BANG!*—it's done.

One time Daniel was praying to the Lord about some things that were hard for him to understand. Suddenly, the angel Gabriel appeared to him. (Angels seem to always appear "suddenly." I've never heard of one that appeared *slowly* or sort of strolled into the room.)

Daniel said,

Gabriel came to me…He came flying quickly to me about the time of the evening sacrifice, while I was still praying. He taught me and said to me, "Daniel, I have come to give you wisdom and to help you understand. When you first started praying, an answer was given, and I came to tell you, because God loves you very much" (Daniel 9:21-23).

As soon as Daniel began praying, God gave the answer to Gabriel and *WHOOOOOSH!*— the great angel flew from Heaven like a golden laser beam. And there he was, standing on Earth, not even breathing hard.

Angels must already know an important lesson for people to learn: The faster we obey God, the happier we will be. The longer we delay doing what we know is right, the heavier our hearts will feel. Someone in the book of Psalms once wrote:

I will hasten and not delay to obey your commands (Psalm 119:60, NIV).

Do you suppose he learned that from an angel?

2. WE CAN LEARN HOW TO WORSHIP THE LORD WITH ALL OUR HEART.

I think angels have been worshiping from the time they first opened their eyes and saw God's smile.

Before there ever was an "Earth," or any people at all, the angels were there, loving God and singing His praises with all their hearts.

Once God was talking to a man named Job about those things. God told Job that when He first rolled Earth into a ball and made it into a world, "the morning stars sang together and all the angels shouted with joy" (Job 38:7).

What did those angels shout, when God sent that beautiful new world spinning and spinning, like a bright blue marble in the blackness of space?

What would *you* have shouted if you had watched that happen right before your eyes?

HE DID IT!

OOOOH! LOOK AT THAT! LOOK AT THAT!

OH—IT'S SO BEAUTIFUL!

GOD—YOU ARE SO WISE!

GOD—YOU ARE SO STRONG!

PRAISE YOUR NAME! PRAISE YOUR NAME FOREVER!

The angels might have shouted things like that, in all their joy and excitement.

Or maybe they just said, "*Wow!*"

Angels are always thanking God for who He is and what He has done. There are even special angels around God's throne who never, ever stop praising His name. They don't have rest time or recess. They don't go home at night because there is no night—and they wouldn't want to leave God's side even if there was. Shouting and singing praise to the Lord is all they do—and all they *want* to do—forever and ever.

Someday, when you and I are in Heaven, we'll get to praise God and the Lord Jesus right alongside the angels. They'll probably teach us a lots of songs we don't know, and maybe we'll teach them a few songs they don't know. Or maybe we'll all learn some new songs together! Until that time, we need to get in practice for Heaven and praise God as much as we can.

The angels love it when we do.

I will hasten and not delay to obey your commands.
PSALM 119:60, NIV

JESUS WILL COME BACK WITH ALL THE ANGELS

"You will see the Son of Man sitting at the right hand of God, the Powerful One. And you will see him coming in clouds in the sky."

MATTHEW 26:64

"*The Son of Man will come again in his great glory, with all his angels. He will be King and sit on his great throne*" (Matthew 25:31).

When Jesus finally comes back to Earth as the great King of Kings, He won't come by Himself! The Bible says He will come with all of His angels. Millions and millions of them. Like a sky full of stars, burning with silver flames.

Of course He would have to bring them *all*. How would you like to be the one angel who got left behind when Jesus came back to Earth in all His beautiful glory? But He isn't going to leave any of the angels behind! All of them get to come.

The Bible also says that Jesus will come back "in the clouds." I wonder….Do you think those will be regular *cloud* clouds…or might they be *clouds of angels*?

What a sight that will be! The whole sky swimming and shimmering with shining, excited angels. And the High King of Heaven and Earth will shine brightest of all.

36

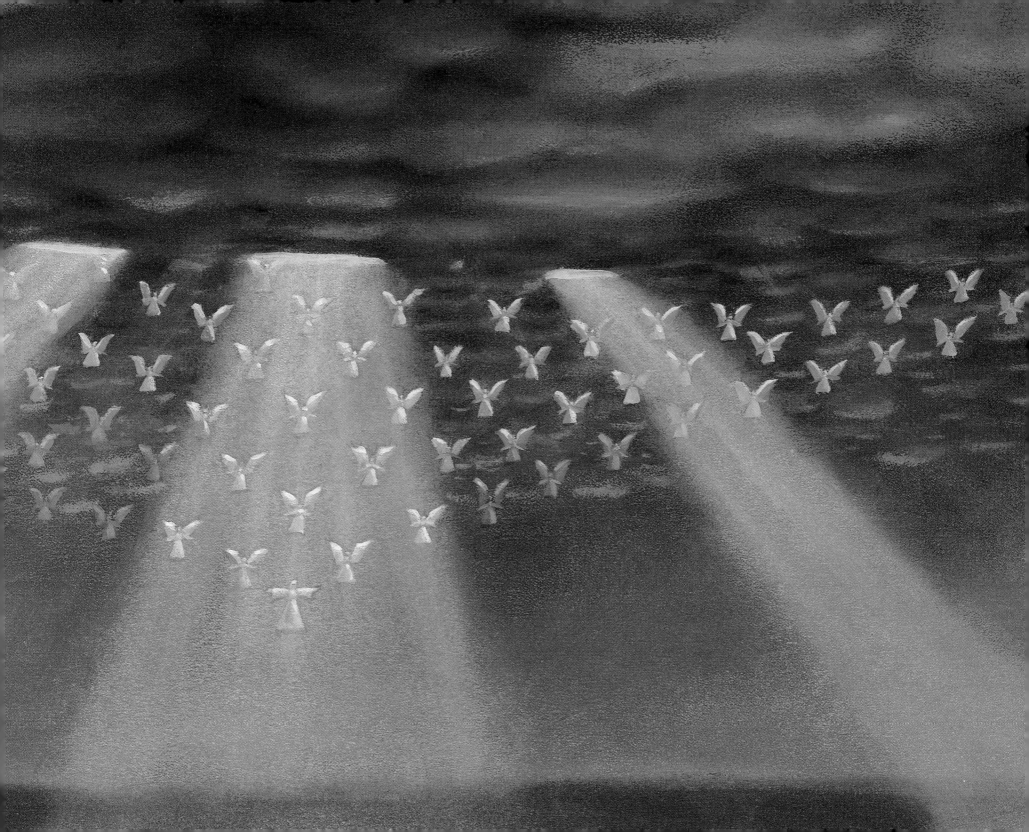

THE NEWS ANGELS LOVE BEST

❧

I tell you there is more joy in heaven over one sinner who changes his heart and life, than over ninety-nine good people who don't need to change…There is joy in the presence of the angels when one sinner changes his heart and life (Luke 15:7,10).

I don't know how news gets around in Heaven, but somehow it does. I don't think there is any need for television or radio or newspapers. When folks in Heaven need to know something, they just know it, that's all.

The Bible says when even *one person* on Earth—one man or woman, one little boy, one little girl—asks Jesus Christ to be Savior and Lord, it's BIG NEWS in Heaven. Jesus tells us that our Heavenly Father's heart fills with great joy when someone on Earth accepts His gift of eternal life. He laughs and sings and celebrates just as…

> a shepherd who finds a lost wandering sheep…
> a woman who finds a lost gold coin…
> a father who finds a lost dearly-loved son.

Angels, of course, are always with the Father and burn with desire to please Him and serve Him. So when God the Father is happy, I think angels must reflect that happiness all over Heaven. (And maybe just a little spills over to Earth.)

Let's just imagine that YOU have said "Yes" to the Lord Jesus.

YES, you know your heart is full of bad things.

YES, you need God to forgive you.

YES, you believe that Jesus died on the cross for all the wrong things you have done, and took the punishment that should have been yours.

YES, you believe He came back from the dead and now lives forever in Heaven.

YES, you give all of yourself to the Lord Jesus, as best you know how.

Did you know that the news of that "Yes" to Jesus just flies across Heaven?

> From street to golden street,
> > from castle to shining castle,
> > > from mountain to towering mountain,
> > > > from cloud to light-splashed cloud,
> > > > > from star to flaming star.

However big Heaven is (and I think it must be *very* big, don't you?), the news is ALL OVER before you can blink an eye.

And you just can't believe how much gladness races across Heaven at such news. It's like one long peal of joyous thunder. It's like a burst of golden fireworks that shines on everyone at once.

Yes, there is joy among the angels when someone (like you) says "Yes" to the Lord Jesus. But I wouldn't be surprised if there are people in Heaven who are happy about it, too…

> grandfathers and great-grandfathers
> grandmothers and great-great grandmothers
> pastors and teachers who loved you once and love you still
> friends who are with Jesus and wait for you to come Home.

Have you said "Yes" to Jesus?

If you have, the angels are still singing about it. If you haven't, there is a party in Heaven just waiting to happen!

38

WILL ANGELS
TAKE ME TO HEAVEN?

❧

No one *I* know likes to go on trips all alone. What fun would that be? Can you imagine riding the front car at Thunder Mountain in Disneyland and having no one to scream and laugh with?

Can you imagine watching the sun set over a still mountain lake, making the water glow like red fire beneath a glass window, and having no one to watch it with you?

Can you imagine peeking over into the wild, solemn beauty of the Grand Canyon, when winter snow clings to the little bushes and red rocks, and not being able to turn to someone and say, "Wow! *Look at that*!"

Most of us don't like to see new places alone.

Most of us don't like to keep beautiful things to ourselves.

Something in us wants to *share* the things that fill our hearts.

Something in us wants someone to *be there*.

That's the way God has made us. Do you think maybe that's the way *He* is, too? Why else would He have bothered making angels and people with eyes to see and ears to hear and noses to smell and hands to feel and tongues to taste His Creation?

Now some fine day, you and I will see Heaven for the very first time.

Some day (not so much different from this day), you and I will just step right out of this life and journey to God's good Home.

That Home will be so very much better than Disneyland and sunsets and mountain lakes and snowy canyons that I can't even tell you how much. And I don't think God means for us to be alone when we travel to that new Home.

Jesus once told a story about a man named Lazarus. He was a man who loved God, but was very poor and lonely and sick. When Lazarus died, Jesus said that angels tenderly carried him to Heaven—where he would never be poor or lonely or sick again.

God sent angels to bring that one poor man from Earth to Heaven. Doesn't that sound like something our heavenly Father would do for us, too, when the time comes to say goodbye to our old life?

I can't imagine Him saying, "Find your own way home, child. I'll leave the light on and the door unlocked. Call Me when you get there."

No, I don't think He is that kind of Father. I think He says, "Just as soon as it's time for you to leave, I will *send someone* to bring you! You won't be alone. You won't be afraid. You won't have to find your own way. And the person I will send knows the way very well."

Why might God send an angel to bring us Home?

First, because He loves us so very much. And maybe second, because He loves the angels, too! Every time an angel brings a man or woman or boy or girl Home, it's a time of deep, heartfelt joy. It doesn't matter if the person is a grown-up who has lived a long life on Earth or the tiniest baby who hardly began to live at all. (Angels, I think, can carry a big football player as easily as a little child. And nobody gets to bring any luggage!)

The time came when the beggar died and the angles carried him to Abraham's side.
LIKE 16:22

41

Why would angels love to do this?

Well, just put yourself in *their* place for a moment. Have you ever shown someone a beautiful place that was very special to you? When I was a little boy, I remember when my grandma from Nebraska first got to see the Pacific Ocean. "Oh *my!*" she said, and her eyes went wide with wonder. It was almost as fun as seeing it for the first time myself!

It must be the same way for the angels.

An angel gets to *be there* when you see the shining beauty of your Forever Home for the VERY FIRST TIME. And when your eyes fly open wide, and your mouth drops open, and the tears of happiness rush to your eyes, and you say, "Oh, my! It's more BEAUTIFUL than I could have dreamed! Is this really my New Home?"—that angel gets to be there to share in it all.

So when it comes to leaving Earth for Heaven, there's nothing to worry about. Children of God never miss the bus. Children of God never wait for the next plane. God wants you Home so much that He'll send His own angel to meet you.

And don't be surprised if that angel is wearing a big smile.